Queens and Princesses

Nefertiti

Katie Parker

Children's Press®
An Imprint of Scholastic Inc.

Content Consultant
Mita Choudhury
Professor of History
Vassar College
Poughkeepsie, New York

Library of Congress Cataloging-in-Publication Data

Names: Parker, Katie, author.
Title: Nefertiti / Katie Parker.
Description: New York : Children's Press, an imprint of Scholastic Inc.,
   2020. | Series: A true book | Includes index. | Audience: Grades 4-6. |
   Summary: "The book explains the life of Queen Nefertiti"-- Provided by
   publisher.
Identifiers: LCCN 2019031652 | ISBN 9780531131725 (library binding) | ISBN
   9780531134320 (paperback)
Subjects: LCSH: Nefertiti, Queen of Egypt, active 14th century
   B.C.--Juvenile literature. | Queens--Egypt--Biography--Juvenile
   literature. | Egypt--History--Eighteenth dynasty, ca. 1570-1320
   B.C.--Juvenile literature.
Classification: LCC DT87.45 .P37 2020 | DDC 932/.014092 [B]--dc23

All rights reserved. Published in 2020 by Children's
Press, an imprint of Scholastic Inc.
Printed in North Mankato, MN, USA 113

SCHOLASTIC, CHILDREN'S PRESS, A TRUE BOOK™,
and associated logos are trademarks and/or
registered trademarks of Scholastic Inc.

Scholastic Inc., 557 Broadway, New York, NY 10012

1 2 3 4 5 6 7 8 9 10 R 29 28 27 26 25 24 23 22 21 20

Book produced by 22 MEDIAWORKS, INC.
Book design by Amelia Leon / Fabia Wargin Design

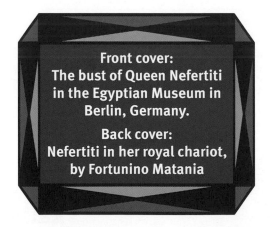

Front cover:
The bust of Queen Nefertiti
in the Egyptian Museum in
Berlin, Germany.

Back cover:
Nefertiti in her royal chariot,
by Fortunino Matania

Find the Truth

Everything you are about to read is true *except* for one of the sentences on this page.

Which one is **TRUE**?

T or F   Nefertiti had six daughters.

T or F   Nefertiti was King Tutankhamun's mother.

Find the answers in this book.

3

Contents

Introduction 6

1 The Making of a Queen

Who was Nefertiti? 8

2 A Religious Revolution

How did religion change
during the time of
Nefertiti? **16**

3 Art Revolution

How was art transformed
during the reign of
Nefertiti? **26**

Akhenaten holding on his lap one of the daughters he had with Nefertiti.

A mask of Smenkhkare, the pharaoh after Akhenaten.

The BIG Truth

The Disappearance of Nefertiti

What are some theories about Nefertiti's sudden disappearance?............**32**

4 Lost to History

What happened to Nefertiti? **34**

Family Tree **42**

True Statistics **44**

Resources **45**

Glossary................ **46**

Index **47**

About the Author **48**

King Tutankhamun

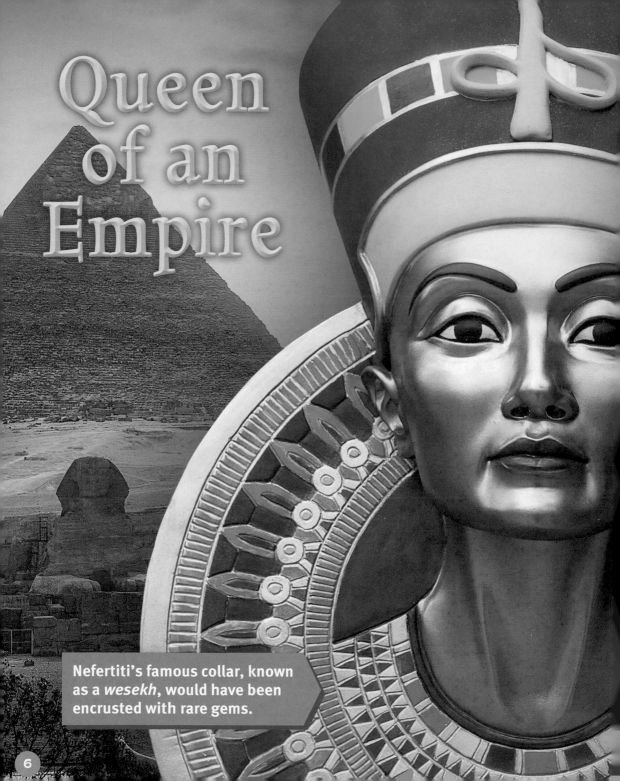

Queen of an Empire

Nefertiti's famous collar, known as a *wesekh*, would have been encrusted with rare gems.

For **thousands of years,** the ancient Egyptian Empire radiated power and prosperity like the world had never seen. Its **pharaohs,** or kings, lived lives of great wealth and unlimited power. **Some of Egypt's greatest monuments were built to honor its pharaohs. The Great Pyramids,** for example, were built as **tombs for these powerful men.** Egyptian queens rarely had the same influence or control. But **one Egyptian queen ruled alongside her husband,** sharing some of his authority. The brief time she spent on the throne was both revolutionary and mysterious. Her name was **Nefertiti.**

The ancient Egyptian Empire lasted more than 3,000 years.

Fertile conditions along the Nile were central to the success of the ancient Egyptian civilization.

The Making of a Queen

Built along the shores of the fertile Nile River, the wealth and culture of ancient Egypt were unrivaled. Egypt produced an agricultural bounty that made the empire a rich trading center. Lavish religious festivals took place throughout the year in major cities, like Thebes, Karnak, and Memphis.

Around 1370 BCE, a little girl named Nefertiti was born into this prosperous world.

The Mystery Begins

Egyptian art often showed gods with the royal family. Here, the goddess Isis leads Nefertiti.

The mystery surrounding this beautiful queen begins with her birth. Who were her parents? Egypt's **scribes** kept intricate records in **hieroglyphics**, a complex system of symbols used for that purpose. They recorded the lives of their royal rulers, inking stories on **papyrus** scrolls or carving them into tomb walls. Artwork and artifacts, including mummies, clayware, and jewelry, have survived thousands of years to reveal Egypt's secrets. But nothing from Nefertiti's childhood can be found.

Some Egyptologists think Nefertiti was born to a royal family in Syria, a neighboring country. The name Nefertiti means "a beautiful woman who has come," which may be a clue that she was not Egyptian.

Others have interpreted ancient records to mean that Nefertiti was the daughter of Ay—one of pharaoh Amenhotep III's trusted advisers—and was raised in the pharaoh's palace. It would explain how she married a prince, when royals almost always used marriage to keep power within their family.

Giant statues like these of Amenhotep III were often built to honor a pharaoh.

From Teen to Queen

Nefertiti's story becomes much clearer around 1355 BCE, the year she turned 15. She was married to Amenhotep IV, the future king.

Two years later, Amenhotep IV became pharaoh. Suddenly, he ruled over a vast Egyptian Empire of about three million people. He inherited wealth amassed over entire centuries. Nefertiti became his queen.

Nefertiti was known by many titles, including Lady of Grace, Sweet of Love, Great King's Wife, and Lady of All Women.

Amenhotep IV, like other pharaohs, often wore a metallic beard to honor and please the bearded god Osiris, whose job was to judge the kings in the afterlife.

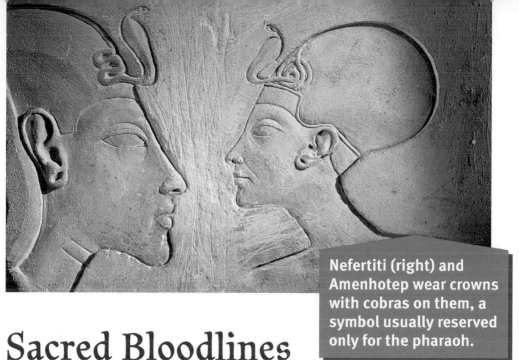

Nefertiti (right) and Amenhotep wear crowns with cobras on them, a symbol usually reserved only for the pharaoh.

Sacred Bloodlines

Ancient Egyptians believed their pharaohs were **divine**—gods in human form. The Egyptians were **devout** in their beliefs. No one dreamed of questioning the pharaoh's word or his ideas.

The pharaoh's children were also **revered**. Pharaohs had several wives, to have more children. In this way, they thought more gods would walk among the Egyptian people. It was an honor for a queen to become "mother of the pharaoh."

Amenhotep IV and Nefertiti's marriage was unusual. While it was probably an important political agreement, artifacts offer clues that Amenhotep and Nefertiti were also in love. **Frescoes** illustrate them embracing each other and their children. Archaeologists even found a **stela,** a monument that marked a city's boundaries, with a poem on it written by Amenhotep, expressing his love for Nefertiti.

Sixteen stelae have been found at the excavation of Amarna, the city built by Amenhotep and Nefertiti.

The Egyptian people were probably surprised to see art depicting the ruling family relaxing.

Ancient artwork reveals another important clue about how unique their relationship was. A drawing on a tomb wall shows Nefertiti seated next to the pharaoh on a throne of equal size. The Egyptian people would have seen this as a symbol of her husband's belief in her ability to lead alongside him.

In some artwork, Nefertiti is even shown smiting enemies in war, like a king!

Amenhotep gave Nefertiti the honor of performing religious ceremonies, unlike any Egyptian queen before her.

In 1338 BCE a total eclipse occurred. It is likely the Egyptians believed they had angered their gods in some way.

A Religious Revolution

By the time Nefertiti became queen, the Egyptian people had practiced the same religion for 2,000 years. The people believed in many gods, some more powerful than others. Elaborate festivals were held to celebrate and honor these gods. The Egyptians believed that when the gods and the pharaoh were pleased, their society would prosper.

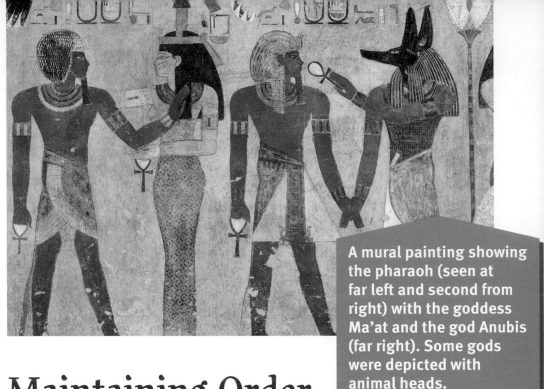

Maintaining Order

The gods of the ancient Egyptians were present in the people's daily lives. Before Nefertiti and Amenhotep IV took power, people dedicated stone temples to gods and goddesses. The Egyptians believed these **deities** lived in the temples. Inside, walls depicted the pharaoh engaging directly with the gods. On festival days, the Egyptian people would take part in the ritual celebrations.

Important Egyptian Deities

These are just some of the many gods or goddesses ancient Egyptians worshipped for thousands of years.

- **AMUN**: The king of the gods
- **ANUBIS**: The god of the dead, the Divine Embalmer
- **ATEN**: The god represented by the sun disk
- **HORUS**: The god of vengeance, protector of kings
- **ISIS**: The protective goddess of magic and spells
- **MA'AT**: The goddess of truth, justice, and peace
- **OSIRIS**: The god of the underworld
- **RA**: The god of the sun and radiance
- **THOTH**: The god of knowledge and writing

Ma'at was often pictured wearing a feather, the symbol of truth, on her head.

From Many to One

Throughout Egypt's history, different pharaohs favored certain gods. Amenhotep IV declared that Aten, a sun god, was the most powerful god. It is unlikely that many Egyptians took notice of this at first or worried about what it meant.

But then the pharaoh stopped giving money to support temples for other gods. Priests who had overseen these other places of worship were once powerful and respected. Now, they were out of a job.

This carving of the pharaoh as a sphinx is one of two that flanked the doors to a temple for Aten.

The pharaoh's next act was to change names. Amenhotep became "Akhenaten" and Nefertiti became "Neferneferuaten-Nefertiti" (notice "Aten" in both names). He ordered Egyptians to abandon their ancient religion in favor of worshipping only the Aten.

The Egyptians were probably confused. How could they choose between their pharaoh and their gods? Did Nefertiti believe in her husband's vision? No one knows. But she continued to appear at his side.

A relief shows the royal couple similar in size, representing their equality.

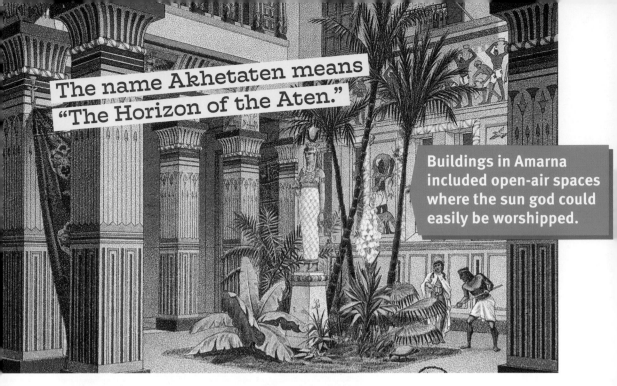

The name Akhetaten means "The Horizon of the Aten."

Buildings in Amarna included open-air spaces where the sun god could easily be worshipped.

The Horizon of the Aten

Nefertiti and her husband began building a new city they called Akhetaten, dedicated to the god of the sun disk. Today, it is known as Amarna.

The city was situated in the desert, far from Egypt's other developed areas. The plans for Akhetaten included a temple just for Nefertiti. This honor showed the world how much influence she had as queen.

A City Rises

Many of Egypt's richest citizens moved to the new capital of the empire. They were probably given lavish gifts to entice them to relocate. Within two years, the pharaoh, Nefertiti, and these nobles were living comfortably in the new city.

The king was feverish in his religious devotion, demanding his city be completed quickly. A workforce of thousands was required to build Amarna. Forced laborers, including many children, were brought in to do the work.

Egyptians worshipping the Aten. The sun god is represented by the sun disk in the painting.

Glorious City

The city of Amarna was built so the **cult** of the Aten could worship the god in peace. The royals spared no expense. The city itself had docks leading right up to the Nile River. At the city's center were temples. The main temple was called the Great Aten. It was huge! There were more than 700 tables inside where food offerings for the Aten were placed.

Nefertiti and Akhenaten would begin the day with a chariot ride from one end of Amarna to the other to symbolize the sun's journey.

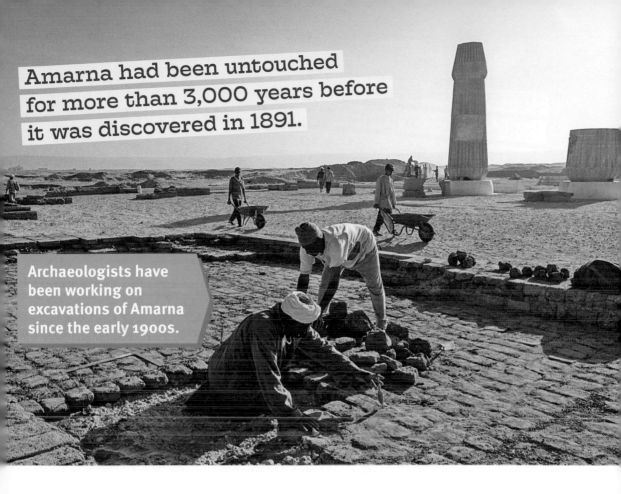

Amarna had been untouched for more than 3,000 years before it was discovered in 1891.

Archaeologists have been working on excavations of Amarna since the early 1900s.

There were palaces for the king and the important people in his court. A small temple within the pharaoh's palace allowed him to worship Aten in private. Palaces to the north of the city were built for his other wives and their children. Nefertiti probably lived in the main palace with Akhenaten.

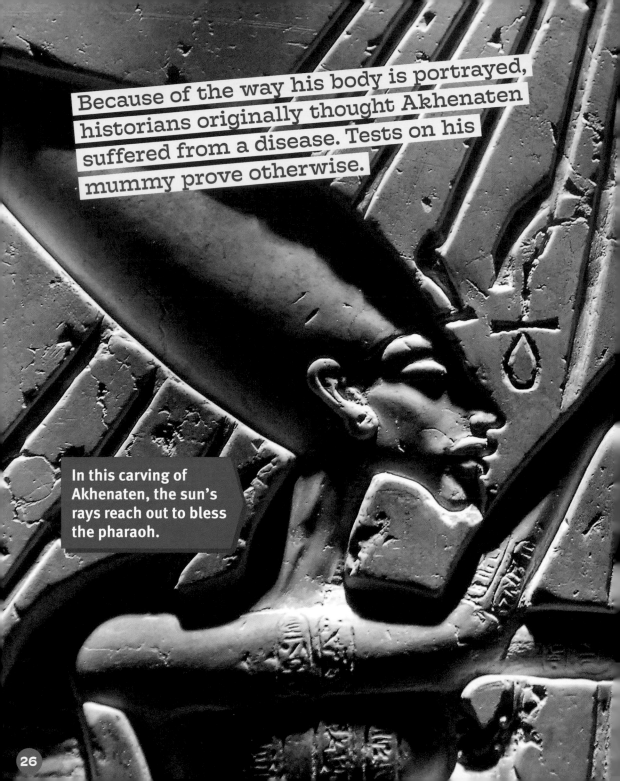

Because of the way his body is portrayed, historians originally thought Akhenaten suffered from a disease. Tests on his mummy prove otherwise.

In this carving of Akhenaten, the sun's rays reach out to bless the pharaoh.

Art Revolution

During the reign of Akhenaten and Nefertiti, not only was religion reinvented, but also art in the ancient world. Suddenly, art pieces showed more intimate scenes. Paintings, sculptures, and drawings on papyrus started to represent bodies in a totally different way. This distinctive style of Egyptian art is known today as "Amarna style." Pieces from this period are easy to recognize and can be directly dated to mid-1300 BCE.

Missing Artwork

Unfortunately, a great amount of Amarna-style art was destroyed over time. Historians have relied on the little that has been found to piece together the puzzle of Nefertiti's life in Amarna. Art that decorated the walls of excavated tombs show us what life was like under Akhenaten's reign. Sculptures and images of the royal family and religious rituals showcase how central Aten had become.

In this painted statue, the pharaoh and his wife hold hands affectionately.

The New Family Portrait

Art from the Amarna period shows how differently Nefertiti and Akhenaten liked to appear to the world. For centuries prior to Akhenaten's reign, pharaohs and their queens were presented in a formal way. The Amarna artwork features more personal images, like this sculpture experts believe is Akhenaten and one of his daughters.

An unfinished limestone sculpture found in a sculptor's workshop during an excavation of Amarna.

Bodies in Amarna Style

In Amarna style, the bodies usually have an odd shape. The royal family members have skinny legs and arms. They also have large bellies and hips, and long necks and heads. It is possible that these were family traits that the artists exaggerated. Other bodily details such as ears and wrinkles are depicted. Feet are clearly shown with toes indicating left and right.

This wall painting from the Amarna period shows two of Nefertiti and Akhenaten's daughters.

Art with Symbolism

Some historians suspect that the royal couple used art to emphasize their closeness with Aten. For example, their stretched-out limbs may have been **symbolic** of sun rays. They may also represent

In this relief from the Amarna period, Akhenaten, Nefertiti, and their family make an offering to the sun god.

the royal couple accepting "ankh," a word meaning life, from the sun god. Akhenaten considered Aten the provider of life and abundance on Earth. The pharaoh and his queen used art to make sure the Egyptian people understood their power and divinity.

The Disappearance of Nefertiti

For 12 years, Akhenaten ruled with his wife Nefertiti at his side, unrivaled by any queen before her. Then, suddenly, she disappeared. She is not pictured in art after about 1343 BCE, nor does her name appear in written documents.

Scholars and scientists have their theories. *Which do you believe?*

Theory #1: Nefertiti continued ruling.

After Nefertiti's disappearance, we know Akhenaten selected an adviser to rule alongside him. There is little known about the pharaoh who then succeeded Akhenaten, other than his name: Ankhkheperure Smenkhkare. Some historians believe that the adviser and the new pharaoh were the same person: Nefertiti! But why would she have hidden her identity?

Smenkhkare

Theory #2: Nefertiti died of an illness.

Did Nefertiti fall victim to a plague that passed through Egypt? Evidence has shown that the black plague may have started in Egypt at this time. But then . . . why wasn't her death memorialized?

Theory #3: Nefertiti was rejected by her husband.

Akhenaten rejected Nefertiti after one of his other wives gave him a male heir—the boy who would become known as King Tutankhamun. But why is Nefertiti painted on Akhenaten's sarcophagus if she was cast aside?

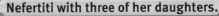
Nefertiti with three of her daughters.

Theory #4: Nefertiti took her life in grief.

Shortly before Nefertiti's disappearance, the royals lost three daughters. Some historians think Nefertiti took her own life in grief. But why was there no record of her death?

King Tutankhamun

Nefertiti was known for her peculiar almond-shaped eyes. The missing piece of quartz that belongs in her left eye has never been found.

The world became entranced by Nefertiti's mysterious beauty once her bust was found.

Lost to History

In 1913, a bust was discovered by German archaeologists during an excavation of a sculptor's studio in ancient Amarna. It was seemingly tossed aside unfinished. Thanks to her identifying headdress, archaeologists determined that the beautiful image depicted was Queen Nefertiti.

The German team took the ancient bust of Nefertiti back to Germany without revealing its importance. Once the significance of the bust was discovered, the Egyptian government began asking for it back, but it has not been returned.

History Erased

The Egyptian people resented that Akhenaten had forced them to abandon their gods. He had tried (and failed) to erase 2,000 years of religion. After his death, Akhenaten was labeled a heretic, someone who goes against the widely held beliefs of the time. And when it came to erasing history... the tables were about to be turned.

After Akhenaten's death, the new pharaoh ordered that the temples and artwork of Nefertiti be destroyed and the palaces disassembled.

Within 50 years of his death, Akhenaten's name was removed from all the historical lists of royal families. So, too, was Nefertiti's name. The city of Amarna was abandoned and many of the **ornate** temples destroyed. Akhenaten's own son, King Tutankhamun, rejected him. He changed

With the discovery of his treasure-laden tomb, "King Tut" became Egypt's most famous pharaoh.

his name from Tutank*aten* to Tutankhamun. This publicly announced the return to a religion of many gods. Tutankhamun's decision showed his people that his loyalty was to them, not to his father.

The Search for Nefertiti

Archaeologists had hoped that once the tombs, or rooms where the dead were kept, at Amarna were opened, they would find the mummies of Akhenaten, Nefertiti, and their children. They also imagined they would find the valuable artifacts most pharaohs were buried with. But there was no sign of the royal family.

Timeline: Discovery of Nefertiti's Family

The tombs of Amarna are discovered. They have rooms for Akhenaten's entire family. But no mummies are found there.

1891

1898

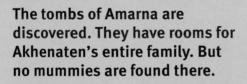

A tomb with three mummies, the "Older Lady," the "Younger Lady" (Akhenaten's second wife), and a child, is found in a side room of a tomb in the Valley of the Kings. One of the mummies is damaged.

Akhenaten's mummy is thought to have been found in 1907 in the Valley of the Kings. Here, about 100 miles south of Amarna, underground tombs designed to keep pharaohs' treasures safe from thieves lay hidden across the landscape. Nefertiti's whereabouts remain unknown.

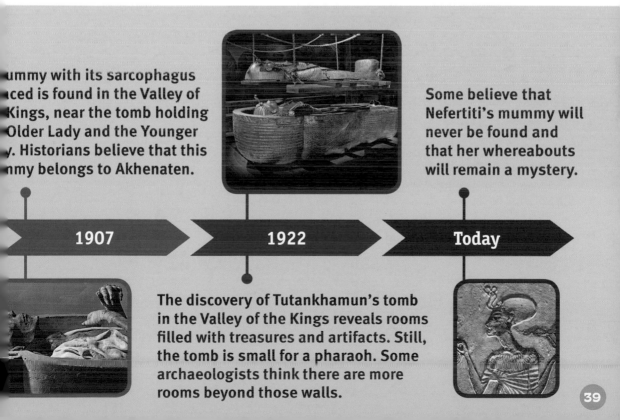

...ummy with its sarcophagus ...ced is found in the Valley of Kings, near the tomb holding ...Older Lady and the Younger ...y. Historians believe that this ...nmy belongs to Akhenaten.

Some believe that Nefertiti's mummy will never be found and that her whereabouts will remain a mystery.

1907

1922

Today

The discovery of Tutankhamun's tomb in the Valley of the Kings reveals rooms filled with treasures and artifacts. Still, the tomb is small for a pharaoh. Some archaeologists think there are more rooms beyond those walls.

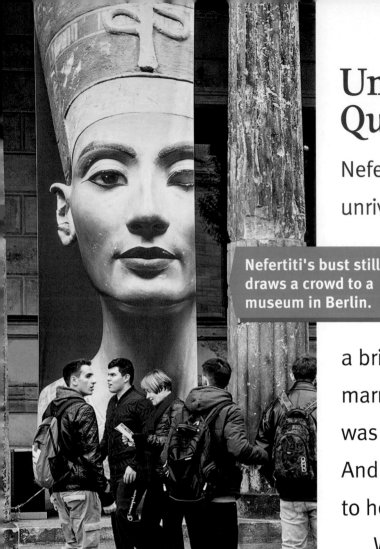

Nefertiti's bust still draws a crowd to a museum in Berlin.

500,000 people a year view the bust of Queen Nefertiti.

Unanswered Questions

Nefertiti's influence is unrivaled for a queen in ancient history. Was she really a brilliant woman married to a man who was ahead of his time? And what happened to her?

We may never know more about Nefertiti, but we will not let history forget such a powerful queen.

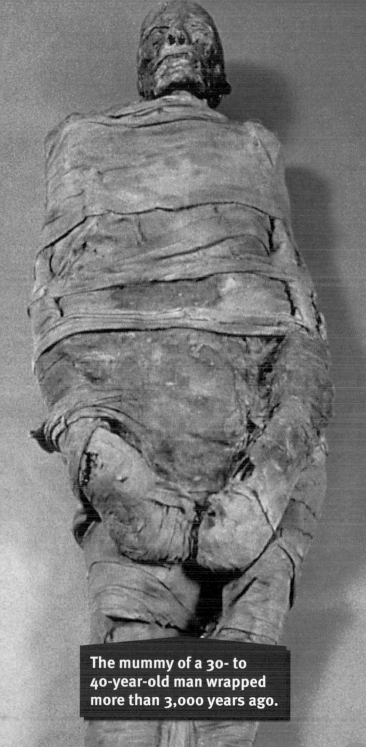

How Egyptians Made Mummies

Preparing a body for death was an elaborate ritual.

Step 1: All the organs were removed, and the body cavity was filled with salt to dry it out. The organs were also filled with salt, wrapped in linen, and placed in protective jars.

Step 2: After 40 days, the body was cleaned and rubbed with oil.

Step 3: The body was then stuffed with rags and carefully wrapped in linen. Wrapping a mummy would take 15 to 20 days.

Step 4: Finally a death mask was placed over the face of the mummy. It was covered with a shroud and placed in a sarcophagus.

The mummy of a 30- to 40-year-old man wrapped more than 3,000 years ago.

Nefertiti's Family Tree

AMENHOTEP III

TIYE

THE YOUNGER LADY

AKHENATEN

The Younger Lady's mummy has double piercings in her ears, just like Nefertiti.

Akhenaten ruled Egypt for 17 years.

NEFERNEFERURE

MERITATEN

TA-SHERIT

TUTANKHAMUN

Tutankhamun was nine years old when he became pharaoh.

NEFERTITI

SETEPENRE

KETATEN

ANKHESENPAATEN

Nefertiti was a powerful queen in ancient Egypt for 12 years. Her bloodline remained on the throne even after her death. Some historians think this may have been her motive in supporting her husband's ideas.

Ankhesenpaaten had two daughters with Tutankhamun.

Approximate year Akhenaten became pharaoh: 1350 BCE

Age of Nefertiti when she became queen of Egypt: 17

Number of children Akhenaten and Nefertiti had: 6

Year the bust of Nefertiti was first displayed in Berlin, Germany: 1924

Years Akhenaten ruled: 17

Years Akhenaten ruled after Nefertiti disappeared: 5

Age of Tutankhamun when he became pharaoh: 9

Year Tutankhamun's tomb was discovered: 1922

Did you find the truth?

T   Nefertiti had six daughters.

F   Nefertiti was King Tutankhamun's mother.

Resources

Further Reading

Ackroyd, Peter. *Kingdom of the Dead: Voyages Through Time*. New York: Dorling Kindersley, 2004.

Drimmer, Stephanie Warren. *The Book of Queens: Legendary Leaders, Fierce Females, and Wonder Women Who Ruled the World*. Washington, D.C.: National Geographic Children's Books, 2019.

Gutner, Howard. *A True Book: Egypt*. New York: Children's Press, 2009.

Hart, George. *Ancient Egypt*. Eyewitness Books. New York: Dorling Kindersley, 2014.

Spirn, Michele Sobel. *Mysterious People: A Chapter Book*. True Tales: Exploration and Discovery. New York: Children's Press, 2006.

Other Books in the Series

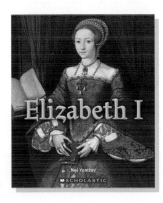
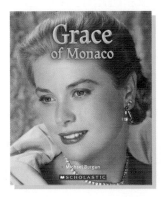
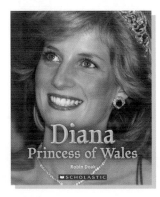

Glossary

cult (kuhlt) a particular form of worship that allows little freedom

deities (DEE-i-tees) gods or goddesses

devout (di-VOUT) devoted, faithful to a religion

divine (dih-VINE) having to do with gods

frescoes (FRES-kohs) paintings on the damp plaster of a wall or ceiling

hieroglyphics (hire-uh-GLIF-iks) a system of writing made up of pictures and symbols

ornate (or-NAYT) covered with a lot of decorations

papyrus (puh-PYE-ruhs) a kind of paper made from the papyrus plant

revered (re-VEERD) honored and respected

scribes (skribes) people employed to keep records by writing them down

stela (STEE-luh) a stone or wooden slab inscribed to commemorate something

symbolic (sim-BAH-lik) standing for something else

Index

Page numbers in **bold** indicate illustrations.

Akhenaten, **21,** 25, **26**–27, **28–29, 31,** 32–33, 36, 38, **42,** 44
Akhetaten, **22**
Amarna, **22**–24, **25,** 28–29, 35, 37, 39
Amarna-style art, 27, **30–31**
Amenhotep III, **11, 42**
Amenhotep IV, **12–13,** 14, 16, 20, **21**
ankh, 31
Ankhesenpaaten, **43**
Ankhkheperure Smenkhkare, **32**
Anubis, **18**–19
art, **12–13, 15,** 27–28, **28–31, 34, 36, 39**
Aten, **20, 23,** 24, 31
Ay, 11

beard, **12**
birth, 9
bust, **34**–35, **40,** 44

chariot, **24**
children, 13, **30, 33,** 44
cobras, **13**

death, 33
disappearance, 32–33

eclipse, 16
Egyptian Empire, 8
equality, 15, 21
excavation, 14, **25,** 29, 35
eyes, **34**

gods and goddesses, 12, 17–21, **18–19**
Great Aten, 24
Great Pyramids, **7**

hieroglyphics, 10

Isis, **10,** 19

Ma'at, **18–19**
marriage, 12, 14
mummy, 26, **39, 41,** 42

name change, 21
Nile River, **8,** 24

Osiris, **12,** 19

parents, 10–11
pharaohs, 7, 13, 20–21

religion, **16**–25, 36
removal of name, 37

scribes, 10
stela, **14**
symbolism in art, 31

temples, 18, 20, 22, 24–25, **36,** 37
throne, 15
titles, 12
tomb, 7, 37, **38–39,** 44
Tutankhamun, **33, 37, 39, 42,** 44

Valley of the Kings, **38–39**

war, 15
wesekh, **6**

Younger Lady, 38, **42**

About the Author

Katie Parker has been putting a lively spin on children's nonfiction and textbooks for many years. She's written books for Barnes and Noble, Marshall Cavendish, Innovative Kids, Capstone, and other publishers.

Katie graduated from Loyola College with a degree in creative writing and psychology. She has pursued adventurous life experiences from riding a camel across the Sahara to studying art in the south of France and working with big cats at Big Cat Rescue sanctuary in Tampa, Florida. Raised in the country, Katie enjoys running in the woods of Connecticut with her family and their dog, Mistletoe.